DANGER! DINOSAURS

DINOSAUR DEFENDERS

Liz Miles

Gareth Stevens
PUBLISHING

Please visit our website, www.garethstevens.com.
For a free color catalog of all our high-quality books, call toll free 1-800-542-2595 or fax 1-877-542-2596.

Library of Congress Cataloging-in-Publication Data
Miles, Liz.
Dinosaur defenders / by Liz Miles.
p. cm. – (Danger! dinosaurs)
Includes index.
ISBN 978-1-4824-3025-7 (pbk.)
ISBN 978-1-4824-3028-8 (6 pack)
ISBN 978-1-4824-3026-4 (library binding)
1. Dinosaurs – Juvenile literature. I. Miles, Liz. II. Title.
QE862.D5 M55 2016
567.9–d23

Published in 2016 by
Gareth Stevens Publishing
111 East 14th Street, Suite 349
New York, NY 10003

Copyright © 2016 Arcturus Publishing

Author: Liz Miles
Editors: Joe Harris, Alex Woolf and Joe Fullman
Designer: Emma Randall
Original design concept: Notion Design

Picture Credits: Key: b-bottom, m-middle, l-left, r-right, t-top. All images by pixel-shack.com except for:
Colin Howard: p 25b. Shutterstock: p11 br; p13 cr; p23 b, 24b, 25t. Wikipedia Commons: p9 br; p17 br.

Printed in the United States of America
CPSIA compliance information: Batch CS15GS: For further information contact Gareth Stevens, New York, New York at 1-800-542-2595.

CONTENTS

ATTACK AND DEFENSE

The age of the dinosaurs was a time of savage battles between hunting carnivores and defending herbivores. Meat-eating dinosaurs had killer attributes to give them an edge. Plant eaters had defensive features such as protective plating, spikes, horns, and powerful, swinging tails.

Some dinosaurs sought safety in numbers by living in herds, just as modern-day grazing animals do. Patterned skin may have helped to camouflage them, and the sheer size of some sauropods would have put off even the most aggressive hunters.

An *Ankylosaurus* swings its heavy tail club to defend itself against a group of hungry *Albertosauruses*.

ARMS RACE

Throughout the long history of the dinosaurs, predators and prey were locked in an arms race, with species evolving ever-improving ways of attacking and defending. As carnivores became larger, stronger, and fiercer, with longer teeth and more powerful claws, so herbivores evolved their own features to avoid becoming a meal. Skin grew thicker, bodies grew bigger, tails grew more powerful, and horns became longer and sharper. The result was some of the most fearsomely defended creatures ever to walk the planet.

↑ WALKING TANK

The herbivorous *Ankylosaurus* (ANK-ill-oh-SORE-us) would probably have put up quite a fight against the aggressive hunter, *Albertosaurus* (al-BERT-oh-SORE-russ). *Ankylosaurus* was covered in a thick shield of bony knobs. Large plates protected its head and neck, and even its eyelids. Four horns at the back of its head warded off biting mouths. Its club-like tail was a defensive weapon that could be swung at an approaching predator. To get a chance of a decent bite, *Albertosaurus* would have had to turn *Ankylosaurus* over and attack it from underneath.

TRICERATOPS
HORN-FACED FIGHTER

Even *Tyrannosaurus rex* (ty-RAN-oh-SORE-us REX) would have found the defensive systems of *Triceratops* (try-SEH-ra-tops) difficult to penetrate. *Triceratops* was one of the huge, four-footed dinosaurs that grazed on plants in late Cretaceous times, and it had to defend itself against some of the most aggressive hunters that ever stalked the Earth.

Built like a giant rhino, *Triceratops* was the largest of the horned and frilled ceratopsians (seh-ra-TOPS-ee-ans).

THREE-HORNED FACE
Triceratops' name means "three-horned face." Its huge head was one-third of its body length. The two horns above each eye were about 3 ft (1 m) long.

SPIKED NECKLACE
The neck plate, called a "frill," was huge and solid, and edged with knobs of bone for protection. The frill may have been patterned to attract a mate. *Triceratops* might have lowered its head to show off the frill, like a peacock displaying its feathers.

CRUSHING TEETH
Triceratops' teeth were built for chomping through vegetation. Rather than chewing, it just crushed, then swallowed.

CHARGE!

If *Triceratops* sensed danger or competition from another male in the breeding season, it may have lowered its head like a rhino or bull and charged. With its truck-sized body weight behind it, the sharp horns would have been deadly weapons. Just the sight of a *Triceratops'* horns and huge frill might have been enough to scare off a rival.

TRICERATOPS VERSUS RHINOCEROS

	TRICERATOPS	RHINO
HEIGHT	10 ft / 3 m	5 ft / 1.5 m
LENGTH	26 ft / 8 m	13 ft / 4 m
WEIGHT	6–12 tons / 5,400–10,800 kg	4 tons / 3,600 kg
SPEED	16 mph / Up to 26 kph	34 mph / 55 kph
NUMBER OF TEETH	400–800	24–34
HORNS	3 horns, 3 ft / 1 m	2 horns, the largest up to 4.9 ft / 1.5 m

FRIGHTENING FRILLS

A bizarre variety of aggressive-looking horns and strange neck plates, or frills, have been found on the heavily defended ceratopsians. A stampeding herd of *Styracosaurus* (sty-RAK-oh-SORE-us) or *Centrosaurus* (SEN-troh-SORE-us) would have scared off most predators. Another defensive tactic may have been to circle the aggressor and slowly close in.

Not all *ceratopsian* frills were large, so some scientists think they were not for protection but for show, and a way of recognizing members of the same herd. Brightly colored frills would have made it easier to identify any competitors that were invading their patch. Other scientists believe that frills weren't used for show, but to help regulate the creatures' body temperatures. Of course it's possible that they had more than one use.

WINNING ON POINTS

Styracosaurus had a horrifying array of spikes and horns. As well as a massive nose horn, it had up to eight spikes sticking out from its neck frill, and a horn protruding from each cheek. There's some evidence that young *Styracosaurus* had two further horns, one above each eye, which fell off when they were adults.

HOLEY HEADGEAR

Ceratopsian neck frills must have been heavy, but *Centrosaurus* had two big holes in the bony structure covered by skin, making it lighter. Moving to get away was perhaps more important for this dinosaur as two of its horns look rather useless – they point down rather than out. However, the long nose horn could have done some damage in a head-butting battle. The vulnerability of the holey frill suggests that it was for display and to deter, rather than to protect. Face-on, the frill would have made *Centrosaurus's* head look bigger than it really was to advancing hunters.

DINOSAUR DETECTIVES

Dinosaur hunters do most of their work with fossilized bones, though occasionally other parts are found. This is a skin impression of a *ceratopsian*. It shows that the skin was made up of small plates, similar to those on a crocodile.

PACHYCEPHALOSAURIDS

BUTTING BONEHEADS

The two-legged, plant-eating pachycephalosaurids (PACK-ee-SEF-ah-low-SORE-ids) are sometimes nicknamed "boneheads." It's possible they may have head-butted each other like goats in fights over territory or mates. This strange tactic was possible because they had a layer of solid, thick bone over the tops of their heads, like crash helmets.

Some scientists argue that the domes must have been for display, not protection, as they would not have been strong enough to withstand being rammed into another bony head or body. The best known of the boneheads from fossil evidence is *Stegoceras* (ste-GOS-er-as).

HEAD-BUTTER
Stegoceras may have used their heads to hit their opponents sideways rather than full-on, so as to avoid serious injury.

BARBED TIARA
A frill of knobs and horns surrounded the domed head like a crown. This might have been for show or for extra protection, or to cause more damage when the creature swiped its head at the enemy.

SHOCK ABSORBER
Scientists have calculated that *Stegoceras's* backbone and neck were strong enough to take the shock of a collision if it rammed its head into an attacker.

THICK HEAD

Pachycephalosaurus (PACK-ee-SEF-ah-low-SORE-us) means "thick-headed lizard," and it is well named – its dome was about 8 in (20 cm) thick. Standing 20 ft (6 m) tall, it was a giant amongst the pachycephalosaurids. Its three types of teeth suggest it probably fed on plants, fruit, and insects.

DINOSAUR DETECTIVES

A tall horn-like crown may have grown upwards from the dome on pachycephalosaurids like an odd sort of wizard's hat. Evidence of blood vessels in the bony domes suggest this possibility. If so, it was probably there for display.

STEGOSAURUS

SAVAGE SPIKER

Stegosaurus (STE-go-SORE-us), a herbivorous, bus-sized dinosaur, had some incredible defensive features to aid its survival. And it needed them, because it lived among some of the biggest and most dangerous hunters of Jurassic times, including *Allosaurus* (AL-oh-SORE-us) and *Ceratosaurus* (keh-RAT-oh-SORE-us).

ROOF LIZARD

Stegosaurus's name means "roof lizard" and this refers to its back plates. It had 17 plates in all, and the biggest was about 2.5 ft (76 cm) tall. The plates may have become brighter in the breeding season to attract mates.

NECK STUDS

The neck and throat are among the most vulnerable parts of the body when it comes to a deadly bite. *Stegosaurus* had bony studs to protect this area.

STING IN ITS TAIL

Two pairs of thorn-like spikes stuck out sideways from the end of its tail – a dangerous defensive weapon that it could swing in the direction of any hunter that got too close.

SLOW MOVER

The back legs of *Stegosaurus* were longer than its front legs. It would have walked slowly with its head close to the ground and its tail held high. *Stegosaurus* could quickly turn around to swing its spiky tail at an unwelcome creature.

TINY BRAIN

Stegosaurus's brain was only the size of a modern dog's, making it the smallest brain compared to body size of any dinosaur. But what it lacked in smarts, it made up for in other ways. Scientists believe it had cheeks – a relatively rare feature in dinosaurs – helping this plant-eater to chew its food properly.

BACK PLATE MYSTERY

There is some evidence that the bases of *Stegosaurus's* back plates were muscular, and it could twist them to face in different directions. No one knows for sure whether the plates were covered in horn and were for protection, or covered in skin and used to regulate *Stegosaurus's* temperature. If they were covered in skin, blood in the plates would have heated up in the sun, then spread to the rest of the body when the warm sunshine disappeared later in the day. If the dinosaur was too hot, the plates could have been used to release excess body heat.

VITAL STATISTICS

STEGOSAURUS

Meaning of name:
Roof lizard

Family: Stegosauridae

Period: Late Jurassic

Size: 14 ft / 4 m height; 30 ft / 9 m length

Weight: 2 tons / 1,800 kg

Diet: Plants

ANKYLOSAURS

DEFENSIVE DEMONS

Ankylosaurs (an-KEY-loh-sores) were bulky herbivores boasting an awesome array of defensive spikes, plates, and tail clubs. They all had thick plating over their backs and scary-looking spikes that stuck out from the sides of their bodies.

MENACING MACE

Like a knight's mace, the bony knob at the end of *Ankylosaurus's* tail could be swung at threatening carnivores. Long bones and powerful muscles in its tail gave it devastating power. Evidence suggests that with a swing of this tail, *Ankylosaurus* could have smashed the bones of any attacking dinosaur.

PROTECTIVE PLATING

Plating would have protected its back, neck, and shoulders. Spiky knobs would have made it difficult for an aggressor to get close enough to flip the heavy monster over and attack its softer underbelly.

BONY EYELIDS

Even *Ankylosaurus's* eyes were shielded. Its eyelids, as well as the rest of its head, were protected by a helmet of fused bony plates (hence its name, which means "fused lizard").

DEADLY CLUBS

The early Cretaceous ankylosaurs, like *Gastonia* (gas-TOE-nee-ah), were small. But by late Cretaceous times, ankylosaurs faced threats from powerful carnivores such as *Albertosaurus*. They became larger and heavier, with defensive plating and deadly clubs at the ends of their tails.

VITAL STATISTICS

ANKYLOSAURUS

Meaning of name: Fused lizard

Family: Ankylosauridae

Period: Late Cretaceous

Size: 5.6 ft / 1.7 m height;
20.5–36 ft / 6.25–11 m length

Weight: Up to 6.5 tons / 5,900 kg

Diet: Plants

BLADED TAIL

Gastonia may have been tormented by the agile, sharp-clawed hunter *Utahraptor* (YOO-ta-RAP-tor), as they lived in the same part of North America. But *Gastonia* had thick plating protecting its neck, back, and tail. And it had a set of blade-like spikes on its tail that would have cut through the air like a knife and done serious damage to any *Utahraptor* that got too close.

HADROSAURS

DEAFENING DUCKBILLS

Hadrosaurs (HA-dro-sores) were duck-billed dinosaurs with huge, hollow crests on their heads. Different types had differently shaped crests, and some looked very bizarre. It seems likely that the crests were used as alarms.

Many scientists think the crests would have been used to make mating calls, to attract other hadrosaurs during the mating season. By varying the amount of air blown through the hollow tubes in its crest, a hadrosaur could raise or lower the volume of the call.

WARNING!

The honking alarm call of *Parasaurolophus* (PAH-ra-sore-OLL-oh-fuss) would alert others in its herd to flee or gather for protection. Although they spent most of their time on four legs, they could run on two legs for short periods when pursued by predators.

SHOW-OFF

The curved head crest may have been brightly marked, either to warn off attackers or to attract a mate. Males and females probably had different sized crests, with the largest on the males.

SLIPPING THROUGH THE FORESTS

By keeping its head raised and resting its crest on its back, *Parasaurolophus* may have been able to create a smooth, streamlined shape. This would have helped it pass through thick undergrowth quickly and quietly. *Parasaurolophus* would have found greater safety in a herd, and even more so if they could move without making too much noise.

HELMET LIZARD

The crest of *Corythosaurus* (core-ith-oh-SORE-us) was shaped like half a plate. This accounts for its name, which means "Corinthian helmet lizard." Its crest looks a bit like the helmet worn by the ancient Greeks of Corinth. *Corythosaurus* also had protective shielding under its body in the form of three rows of scales. These may have been to defend against injury from prickly plants in the undergrowth.

DINOSAUR DETECTIVES

The set of curved hollow tubes in the crest of *Parasaurolophus* were connected to the nostrils. By studying the flow of air through these tubes, scientists have worked out that *Parasaurolophus* could have made a loud and deep trumpeting noise when it snorted through its nose. The hollow tubes probably increased the volume of the call, just as the empty body of a guitar boosts the sound of its strings.

SAUROPODS

TAIL-THRASHING TITANS

With legs as big as tree trunks, size was the sauropods' most important means of protection. A titanosaur such as *Ampelosaurus* (AM-pel-oh-SORE-us) was four times heavier than a predator such as *Tarascosaurus* (ta-RASS-koh-SORE-us). But if hungry, a killer carnivore might still risk an attack, hoping to achieve a fatal bite. Its reward would be a meal that lasted several days.

BULLYING BULK

A predator would normally prefer to stalk weak prey, such as young or smaller dinosaurs, or even hatchlings and eggs, rather than risk being knocked over by the weight of a sauropod. But if hungry enough, a 30 ft (9 m) long *Tarascosaurus* might well take on an *Ampelosaurus*, even though it was massively bigger at 50 ft (15 m) long, and well defended.

WHIP AND STABILIZER

Ampelosaurus's tail could lash out at a pursuer. It could also act as a counterbalance to its weight if it chose to rear up on its hind legs to defend itself.

LIGHT PROTECTION

Unlike the earlier, heavily plated sauropods, *Ampelosaurus* had light shielding. The bony lumps under its skin provided some protection against the mouths of hungry attackers.

SWUNG LIKE A WHIP

Around 90 ft (27 m) long and weighing up to 20 tons, the sauropod *Diplodocus* (DIP-low-DOH-kus) had a very long, 46-ft (14-m) tail that it could have swung like a rope to thrash attackers. Two sets of bones under its tail made it a powerful weapon. When it lashed out with this massive whip, it probably made an intimidating cracking sound.

 # DINOSAUR DETECTIVES

We know that *Diplodocus*'s tail was not so heavy that it had to be dragged along the ground, because there are no tail tracks where *Diplodocus* footprints have been discovered.

PATTERNS AND FEATHERS

For a long time scientists thought that dinosaurs were rather drab and dull looking. However, recent discoveries have changed their minds. Now they believe that many species had patterned skin or brightly colored feathers.

The patterns would have helped to camouflage the dinosaurs, allowing predators to sneak up on prey – and prey to stay hidden from predators.

WHAT COLOR?

We don't know the exact tones or shades of any dinosaur skin, as none of the pigments have survived in fossils. They may have been bright for display, to attract a mate, or warn off a rival.

DISGUISED DUCKBILL

A mummified duckbill has been found, with both skin and bones preserved. The preserved skin shows striped patterns – the first evidence of what a dinosaur skin really looked like and how it may have been camouflaged like a modern-day animal.

WHO WAS IT HIDING FROM?

The hadrosaurs, like the one shown here, were stalked by some of the most dangerous meat-eaters, including the terrifying *Tyrannosaurus rex*.

FIRST FEATHERS

In 1996, a spectacular discovery was made in a quarry in China: the first dinosaur fossil to show evidence of a feathery covering. The dinosaur was *Sinosauropteryx* (SIGH-no-sore-OP-ter-ix), a small meat-eater of the early Cretaceous. The feathers had markings for camouflage or display. By studying preserved pigment cells, scientists worked out that it had rings of orange and white feathers alternating down its long tail, like a tabby cat. Pigments on later dino-bird feathers reveal a range of dark shadings that would have made them very bright.

DINOSAUR DETECTIVES

Well-preserved fossil feathers are a rare find, but some from *Anchiornis* (ANN-chee-OR-niss), a birdlike dinosaur, have been discovered and studied. Through detailed analysis, scientists worked out that its body feathers were black, white and dullish silver, and its head crest was red.

HERDING HEAVIES

There is strength in numbers, and just as modern-day animals gather together to graze, migrate and mate, dinosaurs such as *Protoceratops* (pro-toe-SER-ah-tops) and *Triceratops* would have too. In a group there would have been more watchful eyes and listening ears. If one sensed danger it would run, and the others would follow.

Experts used to think the biggest plant-eating dinosaurs lived alone, especially if they had powerful defensive shielding like *Triceratops*. But evidence has revealed that even these mighty beasts roamed in herds. Areas where lots of bones are found together are the best indication of herds. In one part of Alberta, Canada, hundreds of bones of *Centrosaurus* were found together – evidence of a huge herd, which probably drowned in a flood after a storm.

TITANOSAUR TEENS

It is likely that young titanosaurs would have been protected in a herd. A vulnerable baby would be less likely to be picked off by a predator if surrounded by a mass of giant adults. The fossils of three young titanosaurs were found huddled together. They might have died in a flood, being too young and weak to escape with the adults.

SHIELDED SHEEP

Protoceratops was only the size of sheep and its weak neck plate was just for display. The dinosaurs probably moved in herds because they would have struggled to defend themselves as individuals. We know they were vulnerable because one *Protoceratops* fossil was found with a *Velociraptor* (vel-OSS-ih-rap-tore) skeleton wrapped around it, as if they both died in the midst of battle.

WALL OF HORNS

Like musk ox and other modern-day horned creatures, *Triceratops* could have created a defensive wall by forming a line or circle and facing their attacker together. This would have been enough to intimidate any predator.

DANGER SENSES

Plant-eating dinosaurs needed good senses of sight, smell, and hearing so that they could react quickly to approaching danger. We can tell from their skulls that many plant-eaters had large and well-developed nasal (nose) passages, which means that they could smell predators at a distance. It is likely that hunting dinosaurs had to approach them from downwind.

EYE IN THE SKY

Sauropods such as *Ampelosaurus* would have been able to take advantage of their long necks to keep a look out, regularly lifting their heads high in the air to see far into the distance. They would have also had a major advantage over modern prey animals: the huge predators hunting them would have struggled to hide in vegetation to creep up on them.

360° VISION

Herbivorous dinosaurs needed an all-round view to keep an eye out for danger while grazing. Their eyes were on the sides of their heads, allowing them to see sideways, backwards, and forwards all at once. Killer dinosaurs, such as *Tyrannosaurus rex*, had more forwards-facing eyes like ours, so that they could judge the distance of prey.

DINOSAUR DETECTIVES

There is no way that scientists can measure exactly how good a dinosaur's senses were. However, they can make a good estimate by measuring the shape of hollows in a dinosaur's fossilized skull. They can also make educated guesses based on what we know about animals that are related to dinosaurs. For example, we know that most reptiles and birds have color vision, so we can be confident that most dinosaurs would have had color vision too.

DINO WORLD

Defender dinosaur fossils have been discovered on every continent of the world. The map shows a few examples.

CENTROSAURUS

FOUND IN: Canada
WHEN IT LIVED: Cretaceous
(76–74 million years ago)
Fossils from many different *Centrosaurus* have been found, as well as fossilized impressions of its skin.

STEGOSAURUS

FOUND IN:
North America, Europe
WHEN IT LIVED: Late Jurassic
(156–144 million years ago)
More fossils of *Stegosaurus* have been found than for virtually any other dinosaur. They have been discovered in several states, and one was found in Portugal.

TRICERATOPS

FOUND IN: North America
WHEN IT LIVED: Late Cretaceous
(67–65 million years ago)
Lots of *Triceratops* fossils have been found, including near-complete skeletons. Skin impressions show that it had a bristly tail. *Triceratops* have been found in many states as well as Canada.

ANKYLOSAURUS

FOUND IN: North America
WHEN IT LIVED: Late Cretaceous
(74–67 million years ago)
A complete *Anklyosaurus* has never been found, nor enough evidence to recreate a complete body. The fossils (two skulls and parts of three skeletons) discovered so far were found in Alberta, Canada, and Montana.

AMPELOSAURUS
FOUND IN: *Europe*
WHEN IT LIVED: *Late Cretaceous*
(71–65 million years ago)
Fossils of the huge *Ampelosaurus* have been found in the region of Aude, in southern France.

PROTOCERATOPS
FOUND IN: *Mongolia*
WHEN IT LIVED: *Late Cretaceous*
(85–80 million years ago)
Groups of fossilized *Protoceratops* in Mongolia showed that they probably lived in herds.

SINOSAUROPTERYX
FOUND IN: *China*
WHEN IT LIVED: *Early Cretaceous*
(122–120 million years ago)
Fossil remains of the bird-like *Sinosauropteryx* from China include evidence of the color and pattern of some of its feathers.

Dinosaur defenders came in all sizes, from the towering plate-backed *Stegosaurus* and tank-like *Triceratops*, to smaller heavyweights, such as the waist-high *Protoceratops*.

TIMELINE
OF LIFE ON EARTH

Scientists have divided the billions of years of prehistoric time into periods. Dinosaurs lived in the Triassic, Cretaceous, and Jurassic periods, while modern humans evolved in the Quaternary period.

← CAMBRIAN
541–485 mya: Life-forms become more complex.

↓ SILURIAN
443–419 mya: First creatures on land.

↑ ORDOVICIAN
485–443 mya: Arthropods (creatures with exoskeletons) rule the seas. Plants colonize the land.

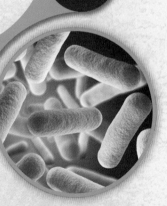

↑ PRECAMBRIAN
4,570–541 million years ago (mya): The first life-forms appear. They are tiny, one-celled creatures.

→ DEVONIAN
419–359 mya: First insects evolve. Fish now dominate the seas.

CRETACEOUS

145–65 mya: *Spinosaurus* and *T. rex* evolve. Dinosaur extinction.

↘ QUATERNARY

2.6 mya- today: Woolly mammoths roam the Earth, modern humans evolve.

← PALEOGENE/ NEOGENE

65-2.6 mya: Many giant mammal species emerge

↓ TRIASSIC

252-201 mya: First dinosaurs.

↑ JURASSIC

201-145 mya: The largest dinosaurs evolve.

↑ TODAY

← PERMIAN

299-252 mya: First therapsids (ancestors of mammals) evolve.

← CARBONIFEROUS

359-299 mya: Reptiles first appear, vast forests cover the land.

GLOSSARY

breeding season Months in the year when creatures gather to mate in order to have offspring.

camouflage Markings or patterns that help something to blend into its setting so that it cannot be easily seen.

Carboniferous A prehistoric period when there were many swamps and forests. Fossil fuels later formed from the trees and plants that died.

carnivore A meat-eater.

ceratopsians A group of large, four-legged dinosaurs, most of which had horns and frills.

crest A body part that sticks up from an animal's head and may be ornamental.

Cretaceous A prehistoric period during which mammals and giant dinosaurs lived, and which ended with the mass extinction of the dinosaurs 65 million years ago.

Devonian A prehistoric period when the oceans were warm and filled with many types of evolving fish.

evolve To change gradually over time.

extinct Not existing anymore.

fossil The remains of a prehistoric organism preserved in rock.

fossilized Made into a fossil.

frill A bony area around the neck of a dinosaur.

grazing Feeding on low-growing plants.

hadrosaurs Plant-eating family of dinosaurs, also known as duck-billed dinosaurs because of their beak-like mouths.

herbivore A plant-eater.

Jurassic A prehistoric period in which many large dinosaurs lived.

plates Bony sections on the surface of a dinosaur that gave it protection. Some plates stood up from the spine, as on a *Stegosaurus*.

predator An animal that hunts other animals to kill and eat.

prey An animal that is hunted by other animals for food.

reptiles Cold-blooded animals that usually lay eggs and have scales.

sauropods A group of giant, four-legged plant-eating dinosaurs with small heads, long necks and tails.

streamlined Something that is smoothly shaped, enabling it to move easily through, for example, water or air.

Triassic A prehistoric period during which the first dinosaurs and mammals evolved.

FURTHER INFORMATION

FURTHER READING

Dinosaur Record Breakers by Darren Naish (Carlton Kids, 2014)

Dinosaurs: A Children's Encyclopedia by editors of DK (Dorling Kindersley, 2011)

Evolution Revolution by Robert Winston (Dorling Kindersley, 2009)

National Geographic Kids: The Ultimate Dinopedia by Don Lessem
(National Geographic Society, 2012)

Prehistoric Safari: Giant Dinosaurs by Liz Miles (Franklin Watts, 2012)

The Usborne World Atlas of Dinosaurs by Susanna Davidson
(Usborne Publishing, 2013)

WEBSITES

http://www.bbc.co.uk/nature/14343366
A regularly updated part of the BBC website, dedicated to dinosaurs.
There is a news section and plenty of cool videos.

http://animals.nationalgeographic.com/animals/prehistoric/
This part of the National Geographic website is home to some fascinating articles about
dinosaurs. There are also some excellent pictures.

www.nhm.ac.uk/kids-only/index.html
The young people's section of the Natural History Museum website. Packed
with downloads, games, quizzes, and lots of information about dinosaurs.

INDEX